FRANCISCANISM

THE ANSWER TO MODERNISM

Bob Sizemore

En Route Books and Media, LLC
Saint Louis, MO 63109

Make the time

En Route Books and Media, LLC
5705 Rhodes Avenue
St. Louis, MO 63109

Contact us at **contact@enroutebooksandmedia.com**

Cover Credit: Sebastian Mahfood

Copyright 2023 Bob Sizemore

ISBN-13: 979-8-88870-110-2

All rights reserved. No part of this book may be reproduced, stored in a retrieval system, or transmitted in any form, or by any means, electronic, mechanical, photocopying, or otherwise, without the prior written permission of the author.

Table of Contents

Dedication iii

Chapter 1: The Profound Influence of St. Francis Always Pointing Toward Eternal Life 1

Chapter 2: The Three Women in St. Francis's Life .. 3

Chapter 3: Water Motif 7

Chapter 4: Franciscanism 11

Chapter 5: Modernism 13

Chapter 6: The Kingdom of God is Within 17

Chapter 7: Living in Community Not Individualism 19

Chapter 8: Illusion vs. Reality 21

Chapter 9: The Enduring Reality 23

Chapter 10: The Final Journey of Life 27

Dedication

To my beloved Franciscan wife, Barbara, and to all Franciscans and would-be Franciscans

Chapter 1

The Profound Influence of St. Francis Always Pointing Toward Eternal Life

Pope John Paul II often looked at the present world and saw in it a "culture of death". There is one saint who looked at the world and promised life, especially eternal life. That Saint is Francis of Assisi.

To talk about St. Francis of Assisi is to talk about a saint who gave the world new metaphors for living. In fact, he has been called the second Christ in the world. He was a saint with a great message.

To change the world means that you have to change yourself first and then lead by example. To put it quite simply, he "left" the world psychologically, but in doing so he enhanced the world by leading a very Christian life.

Chapter 2

The Three Women in St. Francis's Life

How did he accomplish this one very significant way of living? For that answer, we must turn to the three different women in his life. These women would lead all people back to Christ. The women were the Blessed Virgin Mary, St. Clare, his friend and devoted follower, and Lady Poverty, a mental construct, at that time meant to personify what true poverty was all about.

Francis talked to the Blessed Mother constantly. He knew she was the great cornerstone of Christianity. Her saying "yes" to the Virgin birth was held in high regard by Francis, and he created the Christmas Creche that we put under our Christmas trees. For Francis, her acceptance to become The Mother of God he honored as the mystery of the Incarnation. Because of her "yes," God became man in Jesus. She was constantly present to him on both a natural and supernatural level.

St. Clare was his companion and Christian confidant for his whole life. He would exchange ideas with her and always value her advice. With Clare's help, he established the Poor Clare's as the female division of the Franciscans. It is important to remember St. Clare was very powerful in her own right. She helped to bring the masculine and feminine parts of Franciscanism into a formidable group capable of helping both sexes gain eternity.

The third woman, and by far not the least, is someone he called Lady Poverty. She had a tremendous impact on the core of Franciscanism. She is also very multidimensional in providing basic tools to gain heaven.

As was typical of Francis, he personified many things with expressions like brother…or sister… In a sense, his terminology enlarged the Franciscan family by making inanimate or mental objects into people. All were family.

Probably his greatest personification with the most impact is Lady Poverty. To call poverty a lady was indeed a great leap of faith. To encounter Lady

Chapter 2: The Three Women in St. Francis's Life

Poverty, grace filled as she is, became an even greater blessing.

Was Francis really talking about poverty here? Yes, he was, but also talking about much, much, more. He was not denouncing wealth as much as he was elevating poverty to a Christian virtue and ultimately referring to her as The Spirit of Poverty.

There was a theme that everyone could latch onto to gain salvation. It was a master stroke of genius and God's inspiration, which became the sheer essence of what Franciscanism was at core.

Imagine if our world today would fully grasp its significance. It would become a much kinder, gentler world because the personhood and spirit of Lady Poverty would restore balance in the world.

One of the great "tools" Francis has given us is precisely Lady Poverty. She is a lady in poverty who is totally focused on Jesus.

As I have already mentioned, she comes to us as both a person and a spirit. She is the Spirit of Poverty, that deep awareness that if there is any acquisition we need to make on earth, it is the unity of God for eternity. Everything else is illusion. So, we have one man,

Francis, and three highly spiritual females guiding him: Mary, the holy mother of God, Clare, a saint and confidant, and the very powerful Lady Poverty.

Chapter 3

Water Motif

There are some parts of the Bible that have a water motif or background to them. I would like to think that Francis would have gravitated to these passages because water is such an integral part of our lives. Water is also a vital part of our Biblical life. Therefore, I have selected three well-known themes which Francis probably used as teaching and conversion tools.

(1) If you look at a picture or statue of St. Andrew, St. Peter's brother, you will notice he is holding a fish in one hand. Yes, he was a fisherman by profession, and the sea was his domain. But like so many images in the Bible, there are layers upon layers of meaning. Of course, the central meaning here is that Christ said to Andrew and Peter, "Come follow me, and I will make you fishers of men" (M 4, 19). In one poignant moment, the fishing net

(water motif) became a device not for catching fish, but for saving humanity. They will still be fishermen, but in a totally different way. They assented, and the Catholic Church began!

(2) As the Bible continues, we find the Apostles traveling on a boat, at sea, with Christ. He is asleep. Suddenly, a strong storm appears, causing the boat to roll from one side to another. Waves are dashing against the boat. The Apostles were convinced they were going to die. They approached Jesus, pleading with him to protect them from the storm and its dire consequences. Jesus got up and responded by telling the storm to subside. When that occurred, he turned to his Apostles and criticized them for having such minor faith. The message for all ages is that no matter how big the storms are in your life, be they physical, psychological, etc., your personal God will always save you. It is important to notice that the Apostles were

Chapter 3: Water Motif

totally mystified by what happened, saying "Even the winds and the waves obey him" (Luke 8,25). What do we do when our world comes crashing down? The only person who is really in control is Christ, the Savior of the world no matter what the problem.

(3) Before I get fully into the life of St. Francis, I want to continue my water motif with Jesus meeting the Samaritan woman at the well. The woman went to draw water from a well in her Samaritan town. Christ was sitting there by himself, having sent his Apostles ahead to get provisions in town. Jesus was very thirsty after his journey. As the woman was drawing water, Jesus asked for a drink. She hesitated and reminded Him that Jews and Samaritans don't get along, especially a Jewish man and a Samaritan woman. This was not done in her society. Jesus breaks through the seeming problem by saying to her, if she only knew who was asking this of her, she would probably say yes! Jesus continues by saying I have

the power to provide you with everlasting water, which never ends. It was then she became aware that He was the promised Savior of Israel. Once again, water plays such an important part in Christian Salvation.

After the Resurrection of Christ, there were two discernible gifts given to humanity. The most immediate gift was the coming of the Holy Ghost upon the Apostles. God realized that humanity needed continued help to sustain Christianity. It was a great and powerful message sent in the personhood of the Holy Spirit.

Chapter 4

Franciscanism

The second gift of God was to send to the world someone who would be called "THE SECOND CHRIST". The Apostles' boat may no longer have Christ in it, but it would have as close as a human can get to Christ. His name is St. Francis of Assisi, who would further transform the world. His followers grew exponentially to be known as Franciscans.

St. Francis brings us back to what is real, holy, and everlasting in our lives. Modernism, as we shall see, is only interested in what is temporary, what is fantasy, what is surreal, and only what can be transitory.

Francis was all about what is essential in life for us as creatures of God. He was all about learning more and more about the journey within, where God really resides. Francis wants us to become more and more Christ-like and less and less the machine or world-like. He came to quiet the world, which continues to spin more and more out of control each day.

He never emphasized the newest product available, but rather the next relationship available, especially with God who loves us so much.

To get to the essence of the Franciscan message, we must go back to an emphasis on poverty which is Lady Poverty or poverty of spirit. Was Francis really talking about poverty here? Yes, he was, but he was also talking about something that was much more fundamental in the person of Lady Poverty, who represented poverty of spirit. Here was a theme that everyone could latch onto to gain their salvation. It was a formula he was giving us for our own eternity. It was also a master stroke of genius and God's inspiration. Imagine if our world today would fully grasp its significance. It would become a kinder, gentler world because the spirit of Lady Poverty would lead us directly to the Holy Spirit. There would finally be balance in our world. I have deliberately repeated the message of the Spirit of Lady Poverty because it needs constant repetition.

Chapter 5

Modernism

What is modernism? It's how we handle our affairs, where we place our values, how we conduct our lives and where we place our faith in life. What is the end result of modernism today? For many people it is almost a visceral sense that they are moving too fast! We see this in burnout, mental illness, heart attacks, drug addictions and even forced early retirement. In other words, we don't have a human existence as much as we have a machine existence. Let's be clear here, with the coming of A.I., artificial intelligence, we will see a machine age emerge beyond our comprehension.

Computers, etc., will have the power to think and most importantly to be aware more quickly than the human brain. The obvious result is that they will control us rather than vice-versa.

A.I. plays right into our world society to do things faster and faster. We are already going too fast for our own mental health to handle. Information is the currency of the world economy.

If a particular society doesn't have certain information, it will find a computerized way to steal it.

In a sense, the covid epidemic showed us in real time how rapidly all of the world can be affected by a virus. As bad as covid was, the recent information about artificial intelligence indicates a machine world is coming into existence that can control our entire existence. In the hand of an "evil empire," the repercussions are almost unimaginable. To put it in very simplistic terms, humans are discarding what held the world together by common sense in favor of machines which will be powered in a totally unrestricted way. It is as if evolution has brought humans all this way, only to have our own creations, not us, continue to evolve.

Where is our privacy or even our personhood in this mechanistic society? The answer is it's almost non-existent. This extends to medical records, finances, and mental health information.

For the sake of "utopia," we hurtle toward this society not of beings but of non-beings. In the midst of

Chapter 5: Modernism

this activity on earth, our attention is being constantly diverted to outer space—UFO's aliens and exploring planets as if this was the new "Holy Grail" of our generation. What is on Mars or the moon that clamors for our attention? There is nothing but rocks, sand, and gases. The only true spaceship in our life is this wonderful abundant planet called earth.

Chapter 6

The Kingdom of God is Within

Francis, Clare, and the Franciscans call us back over and over again. Christ came to this earth to save us. He also stressed that the kingdom of God is within! It's as if modernism is trying each day to sever the umbilical cord of our church. In our capitalistic system, success and work are decided by how many "toys" you have accumulated and how much status you can claim. How can we put the brakes on this head-long rush toward non-existence that is our own making. We already have the answer that we desperately need. All we must do is to look toward Franciscanism as an ultimate answer to human subjugation or obliteration. The experts have it all wrong. The common people, the marginalized, have it all right! We as humans must live our entire lives to the fullest by simply following the blueprints that Francis and Clare hold in their hands. Jesus, God, walked this earth to save humans because they needed saving.

Whatever tools humanity develops, no matter how sophisticated, will not satisfy the human heart.

The unsaid commentary is you don't have relationships with machines. They are only the newest 'golden calf" humanity has created. You only have relationships with people and with our God/Man Jesus. Relationships are the firm glue that keeps all of humanity together, both now and for those who believe, in eternity.

Modernization is no more than a giant existential storm buffering our rowboats of life. It can only be tamed by a full return to our Christian tradition. The world needs another path to follow. Franciscanism is that path.

Chapter 7

Living in Community Not Individualism

There are two other issues worth mentioning. The first is "meism," for what I want that drives so much of our lives. Couple that with greed, avarice, and a willingness to be controlled by the larger economic system, now through A.I., and you have a formula for disaster.

We are still creatures who have "just" emerged from our ancestral tribalism with the same tenacity they used for survival and dominance. But to survive, to truly survive, we need different evolutionary attributes. We desperately need to live in community. This is where Francis and Clare come into view and provide us with a totally different paradigm. Their message is, we are the Good Samaritans, and we can emerge from this chaotic world if we only follow the simple, all-giving and all-caring life of Francis and Clare. This is life as Christ envisioned it for us.

On the other hand, modernism calls us to dominance because of our extreme egotism. We are literally choking in our own clinging to the price this world demands of us.

Chapter 8

Illusion vs. Reality

The one area I haven't really touched upon which underlies modernism is the distinction between illusion and reality. Never before in the history of the world has this distinction been so razor thin and purports to make illusion a reality.

The beauty of Franciscanism is that it only deals with reality, specifically ultimate reality. That reality is so profound because most people are confused at the simplicity of Francis' life with his message about being Christ-like. The language used by Franciscans is much more a language used in heaven. That is, the language of silence and pure listening.

Here we are on earth perpetuating our hunter-gatherer ancestors, going out every day, not after the kill, but after more and more acquisitions to set us apart from the rest of humanity.

We over-invest our precious time on this earth in things! So, what if we landed a man on the moon? So what? We continue to boast of our accomplishments!

But think of what a greater momentous event it was that God sent His only Son to live on this earth. Is it no wonder that Francis always celebrated The Incarnation as such a momentous event.

Instead of eternity, we pursue the newest, the biggest and the brightest—mere trinkets in what is the true reality of our existence. We need constant reminders that we are not on the narrow path to heaven. Just as a farmer needs to prune his trees periodically, we need to do the same thing with our lives.

This is where the saints excelled. They remind us over and over again that the true living on earth is always done with a constant gaze toward heaven.

Chapter 9

The Enduring Reality

The Franciscans were sent to all of us as a stark reminder of how we need to live our lives. It's all about letting go of things and letting God in to provide us with the grace we need to have complete union with our Creator.

Let me reiterate at this point, one of the great "tools" Francis has given us is Lady Poverty. She is a marvel of both God's grace and the insight of Francis.

Francis goes further with this complex entity. She is the spirit of poverty, that deep awareness that there is nothing to hold onto on earth. Rather, it is eternity which makes everything else pale by comparison. Francis has many other answers to our daily existence—prayer, sacrifice, chastity, and above all obedience to keep our wayward human tendencies in check.

We are all called to sainthood. However, given our own infirmities and weaknesses, we need someone to lead us. Francis is that person, and Franciscanism is the road map to get there. What do I mean by way? As a secular Franciscan myself, I am very familiar with that way. The way is divided into two parts. In its simplest form, it is the small gestures we make in Christ's name: a compliment, a cup of coffee, or offering a ride to the doctor for an elderly patient. Just going to a grocery store and shopping for an infirmed individual exemplifies the Franciscan way.

At an even higher level, it is engaging in prayer for someone. It isn't just prayer but on-going prayer for a particular intercession. Prayer is one of the most powerful things we can engage in at all times. The Holy Rosary is Mother Mary's favorite prayer. Lastly, going to confession and receiving Holy Communion both elevate our own spiritual life and that of the person that we are praying for.

We certainly pray for the living, but we are required to pray for the dead in purgatory to release them from their sins and allow them to gain haven. The Franciscan way is prayer, prayer, and more prayer by ourselves or in groups. When we do pray, we acknowledge who God is and who we are!

Chapter 9: The Enduring Reality

Franciscanism is particularly relevant to the elderly. Here again, modernism holds them in low esteem, especially due to retirement. Franciscanism goes in the opposite direction. It takes the time to be with the elderly, right here, right now. The influence of Franciscanism goes down to the basic building blocks of life and the church—mainly families and couples. In the United States, families have been pulled apart by divorce. [At least one out of four marriages end in divorce.]

Concurrently, separations are also very high. This extends to all age groups whose development depends on an intact family. Even people from 50 to 90 are affected by divorce and may resort to addictions and drugs leading to premature death. If we just concentrate on married couples today, there is violence, abuse, neglect, and assaults in an institution that is suppose to provide emotional security and love.

Chapter 10

The Final Journey of Life

Franciscanism goes to the heart of these problems. It talks about forgiveness, love of your child and spouse, patience with each other, and the holy centrality of the family to our Christian existence. Francis had such an affinity to the Holy Family that his examples of love, sacrifice, and caring really reflect the Biblical message. Francis teaches us it's not about me. It's about you and you and you. As Francis taught us, we must recede into the background of existence and be there for the other. Francis, by his example of praying, saying the Holy Rosary, and receiving Holy Communion prepares us for our final encounter with death. Death is not so much the dramatic scenes one sees in the media. Rather, it can be a joyous end to a life well-lived. As a friend of mine, who used to volunteer at Hospice, once said to me, "People die the way they live." There are few death-bed conversions.

Francis and Clare lead the way as examples of a life well-lived. They spent most of their days living on earth, but at the same time in God's very presence. Francis was not tethered to this earth as so many people are who engage in modernism. His life was totally with God.

If the world only knew what Francis knew, that this life is totally transitory, we would all acknowledge God's holy grace and His glory to come.

I have a room where I store my books. On one wall, I have a picture of my grandfather, Michael, taking me at age 9 or 10 back to shore after a day of fishing (water motif) off Branford, Connecticut.

At the shore, the rest of my immediate family are waiting—my mother, Mary, and my sister, Beverly.

As I look at the picture today, I see superimposed on it, God the father instead of my grandfather, steering the boat toward my eternal shore, heaven. I am now at age 81, with silver hair, waiting to reach my destination. On the shore are all my relatives at least four or five generations deep.

In this, my final water motif, they are waiting for me to land and cheering at the same time. The happi-

Chapter 10: The Final Journey of Life

ness I feel is unprecedented for I have gained my final, eternal Franciscan home. It is an end, but also a glorious beginning. Life has always been about grace, prayer, and holiness. Always!

www.ingramcontent.com/pod-product-compliance
Lightning Source LLC
Chambersburg PA
CBHW070049070426
42449CB00012BA/3197